THE BOY WHO DREAMED BIG

By ALTON CARTER

Illustrations by JANELDA LANE

The Boy Who Dreamed Big

Published by Monocle Press, a division of Strata Leadership, LLC
11600 Broadway Ext. Ste 220, Oklahoma City, OK 73114
www.monoclepress.com

Design by Qubit Creative

JNF002000 JUVENILE NONFICTION ADVENTURE & ADVENTURES
JNF007050 JUVENILE NONFICTION BIOGRAPHY & AUTOBIOGRAPHY

978-1-7321189-6-6

This book is dedicated to all the teachers, counselors, coaches, school administrators, and many others who inspire others to

DREAM BIG

and change the world.

Dream big

Dream big

Set your goals high

Keep your feet on the ground
and reach for the sky

Believe in your dreams

and they will come true

Always believe

YOU

are somebody, too

A dream is a vision
surrounded by inspiration

Hold on to your dream
and fulfill your destination

WELCOME

Reach out for your dreams
when things seem rough

Follow your dreams
when life gets tough

Dream you're a politician
writing a bill

Dream you're a carpenter
using a drill

Dream you're an officer
saving the day

Dream you're a farmer
hauling hay

Dream of reading a book

or

walking on the beach

Dream you're the President giving a speech

Dream you're a parent
a librarian
or teacher

Dream you're an author
a dentist
or preacher

Dream of riding a bike
or watching a bird fly

Dream you're a pilot
soaring through the sky

Dream you're a doctor helping a child that's ill

Dream, Dream, Dream

WHAT YOU WILL!

Inspiration
Using your gifts and talents in a way that makes others feel special

Destination
A place that people will work hard to get to

Dream
Thinking about the possibility of doing something that will make the world a better place

Success
When anyone sets a goal and reaches it

Vision
The ability to see the good in yourself when you feel down

Surrounded
To have positive people all around you

Fulfill
Not letting obstacles stop you from reaching your goals

If you look closely at the illustrations, you'll find 10 cleverly hidden objects that inspired Alton to Dream Big:

- Book
- Candy bar
- Whistle
- Football
- Brick
- Basketball shoes
- Bale of hay
- Dollar bill
- Watch
- Bolt

Can you think of 10 things
that inspire you to Dream Big?

We invite you to draw yourself
doing something that inspires you to

Dream Big!

When the picture is complete,
send a copy to
www.theboywhodreamedbig.com
so we can share it with the world!

Printed in the USA
CPSIA information can be obtained
at www.ICGtesting.com
LVHW052302160124
768957LV00017B/77

* 9 7 8 1 7 3 2 1 1 8 9 6 6 *